Copyright © 2021 by Gahmya Drummond-Bey

All rights reserved.

ISBN: 978-1-7379693-0-3

Published by Evolved Teacher Press.

No part of this publication may be reproduced, stored, or transmitted in any form or by any means, electronic, mechanical, photocopying, recording, scanning, or otherwise, except as permitted under Section 107 or 108 of the 1976 United States Copyright Act, without the prior written permission of the author. Requests to the author and publisher for permission should be addressed to the following email: gahmya@evolvedteacher.com

Limitation of liability/disclaimer of warranty: While the publisher and author have used their best efforts in preparing this guide and workbook, they make no representations or warranties with respect to the accuracy or completeness of the contents of this document and specifically disclaim any implied warranties of merchantability or fitness for particular purpose. No warranty may be created or extended by sales representatives, promoters, or written sales and materials.

Due to the dynamic nature of the Internet, certain links and website information contained in this publication may have changed. The author and publisher make no representations to the current accuracy of the web information shared.

> I am so **proud** of you for picking up this book! One day, you will be an author and **someone will read your book!** Wow!

# Welcome to My Favorite Pets

*My Favorite Pets* encourages young writers to learn new vocabulary, while teaching them a system for writing ideas clearly and with great detail.

Created by an award winning American curriculum designer and teacher, this system comes straight from our English kindergarten in South Korea, where our lovely beginner level writers, ranging from five to eleven years old, learned to write beautiful paragraphs in English.

We teach our students the outline of a great piece, but we also encourage them to use their own ideas.

Best of all, this book encourages fun! Check out our website for the fun digital course that you can take with this book!

With Love,

Gahmya

www.kidYOUniversity.com

**Hello There! I'm Allahna!**

In this book, you will learn about some really cool animals!
You may have one of these animals at home!
Some of the other animals may be new to you!
You will also learn how to write a short paragraph from what you've learned!

Writing a paragraph is awesome.
Books have paragraphs of ideas.
When you learn how to write your ideas clearly, people can read them all over the world!
First, let's learn about what a paragraph is and how to write one!
Meet my friend, Miss Hamburger.

# My Favorite Pets

Written by Gahmya Drummond-Bey

Illustrated by Rustom Pujado & Sidney Lander

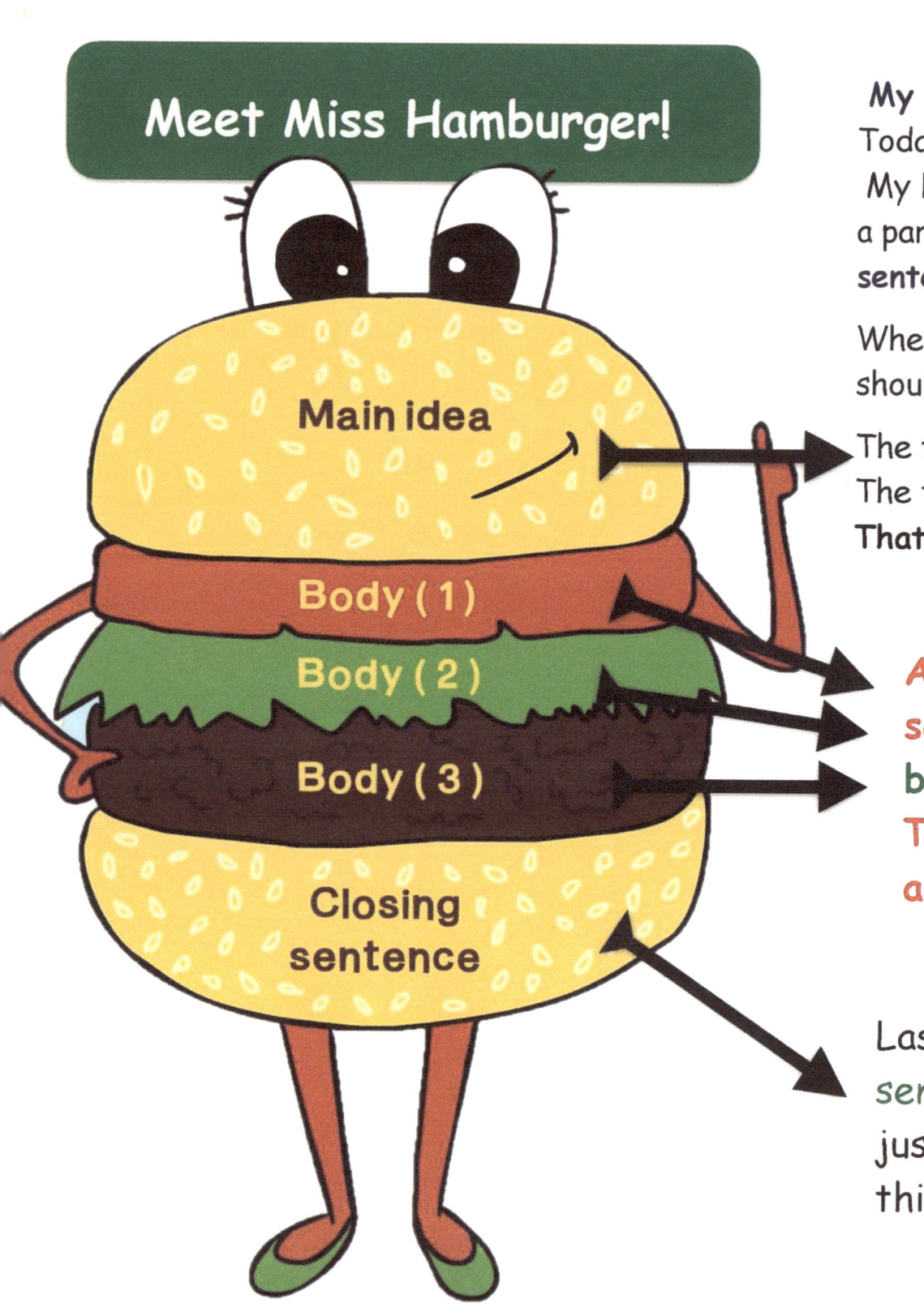

## Meet Miss Hamburger!

- Main idea
- Body (1)
- Body (2)
- Body (3)
- Closing sentence

My name is Miss Hamburger! Today, I wore my special hamburger dress. My Hamburger dress helps you to remember what a paragraph is. **A paragraph is a group of sentences that tell about one idea.**

When you first begin to write a paragraph, you should have 5 sentences. This is a short paragraph.

The first sentence is your topic sentence. The topic sentence tells the **main idea.** That's what you're writing about!

**After that, you have 3 more sentences that are called body sentences. The body sentences tell "Why" and "How."**

Last, we have our closing sentence. The closing sentence just tells the reader what you are thinking one more time!

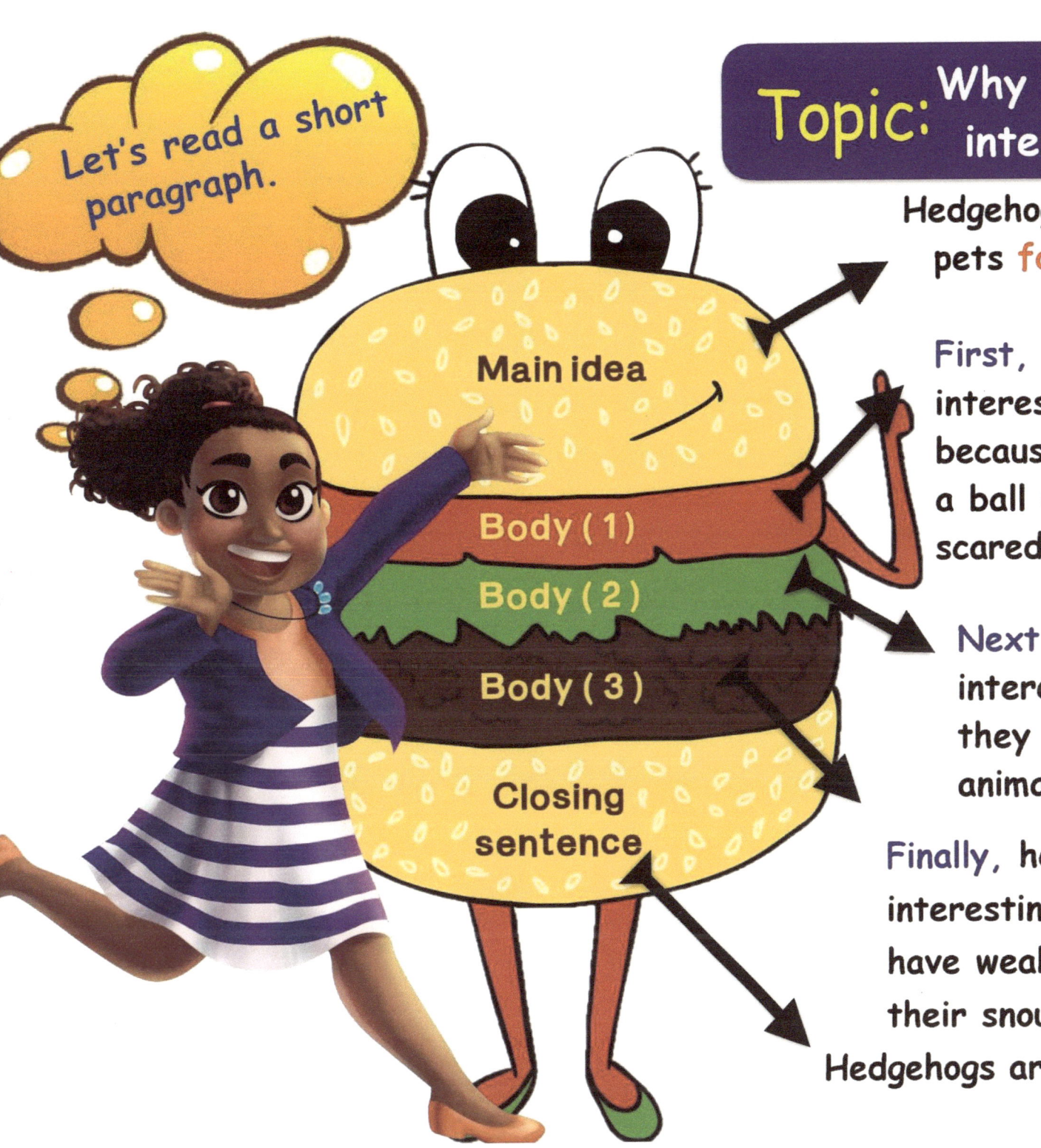

The topic sentence tells the reader what you will write about.

## The topic sentence has 3 magic words: **for many reasons**.

"For many reasons" means that you will tell "why" more than once.

 Why are owls interesting?

Owls are interesting **for many reasons**.

 Why are frogs special?

Frogs are special **for many reasons**.

 Why are horses cool?

Horses are cool **for many reasons**.

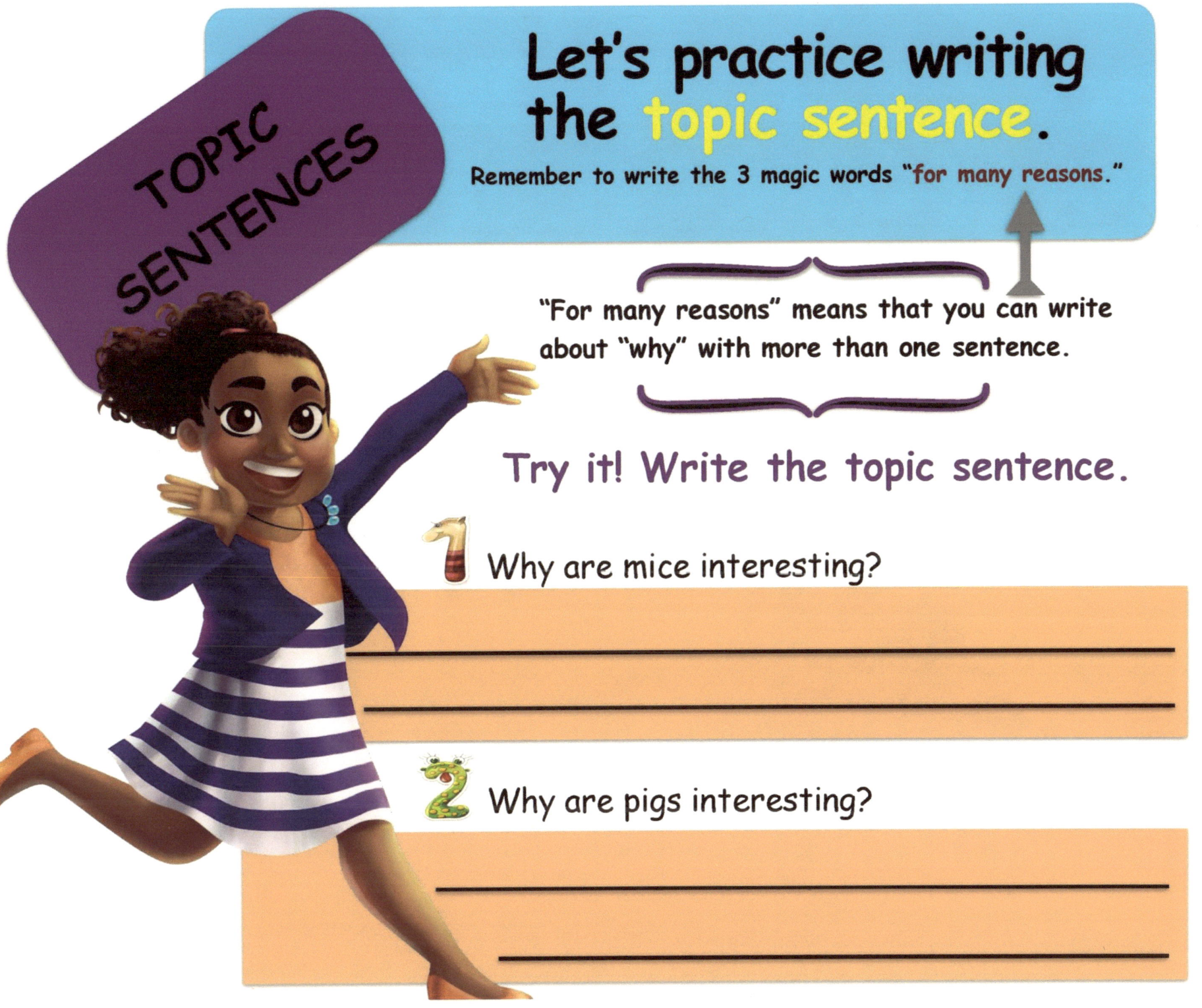

# Why are Guinea Pigs Interesting?

Guinea pigs are from South America. A guinea pig has two names. Some people call it a "guinea pig" and other people call it a "cavy." A baby guinea pig is called a pup. Guinea pigs do not like to get a lot of sleep. So, they take short naps throughout the day. Guinea pigs are not pigs! But, they make squeaky noises that sound like pigs. Guinea pigs are herbivores! That means, they do not eat meat. Guinea pigs like to eat hay and fresh grass. Some guinea pigs also like carrots and broccoli!

Guinea pigs are interesting for many reasons.
_____
_____
_____

First, guinea pigs are interesting because they have two names.

Next, guinea pigs are interesting because they do not get a lot of sleep.

_____ are interesting because _____

DRAW

Draw Guinea Pigs in their Natural Habitat.
An animal's habitat is where it lives.

Wild guinea pigs like to live in groups called herds. They like to look for food together. Their natural habitat is the mountains in South America.

# Word Search

Can you find the words? Circle each word in the word search.

| | | | | | | | | | |
|---|---|---|---|---|---|---|---|---|---|
| g | u | i | n | e | a | p | i | g | s |
| r | n | a | c | l | m | u | l | r | q |
| a | i | g | a | g | e | p | o | o | u |
| s | c | e | r | m | r | p | v | w | e |
| s | o | m | r | e | e | y | e | y | a |
| h | r | u | o | a | z | r | g | v | k |
| o | n | r | t | t | i | f | i | a | y |
| p | e | t | s | h | c | u | o | c | n |
| p | b | r | o | c | c | o | l | i | a |
| e | r | o | v | i | b | r | e | h | p |

**word list**

- guinea pigs
- south
- America
- squeaky
- carrots
- cavy
- pup
- nap
- herbivore
- broccoli
- pets

# Table of Contents

 Let's learn about hamsters.

 Let's learn about betta fish.

 Let's learn about pugs.

 Let's learn about rabbits.

 Let's learn about bengal cats.

 Let's learn about box turtles.

 Let's learn about parrots.

 Let's learn about hermit crabs.

# 1 HAMSTER

Hamsters are rodents.
Rodents are small mammals, like mice and beavers.

Wild hamsters live underground in the daytime, so bigger animals cannot catch them.

Hamsters are omnivores.
They eat seeds, fruit, and insects.

Hamsters have little pockets in their mouths. Hamsters put food in their pockets and carry the food underground to their homes.

Hamsters' eyes are weak. They are also colorblind. That means that hamsters cannot see all of the colors that you can see.

Many people like to have hamsters as pets. Most hamsters live to be 4 years old.

**Lesson 1:**

## Why are hamsters interesting?

Try to write the topic sentence.

_____

_____

_____

Did you write the three magic words?

# Now, read about hamsters again.
# Write 3 reasons why hamsters are interesting or cool!

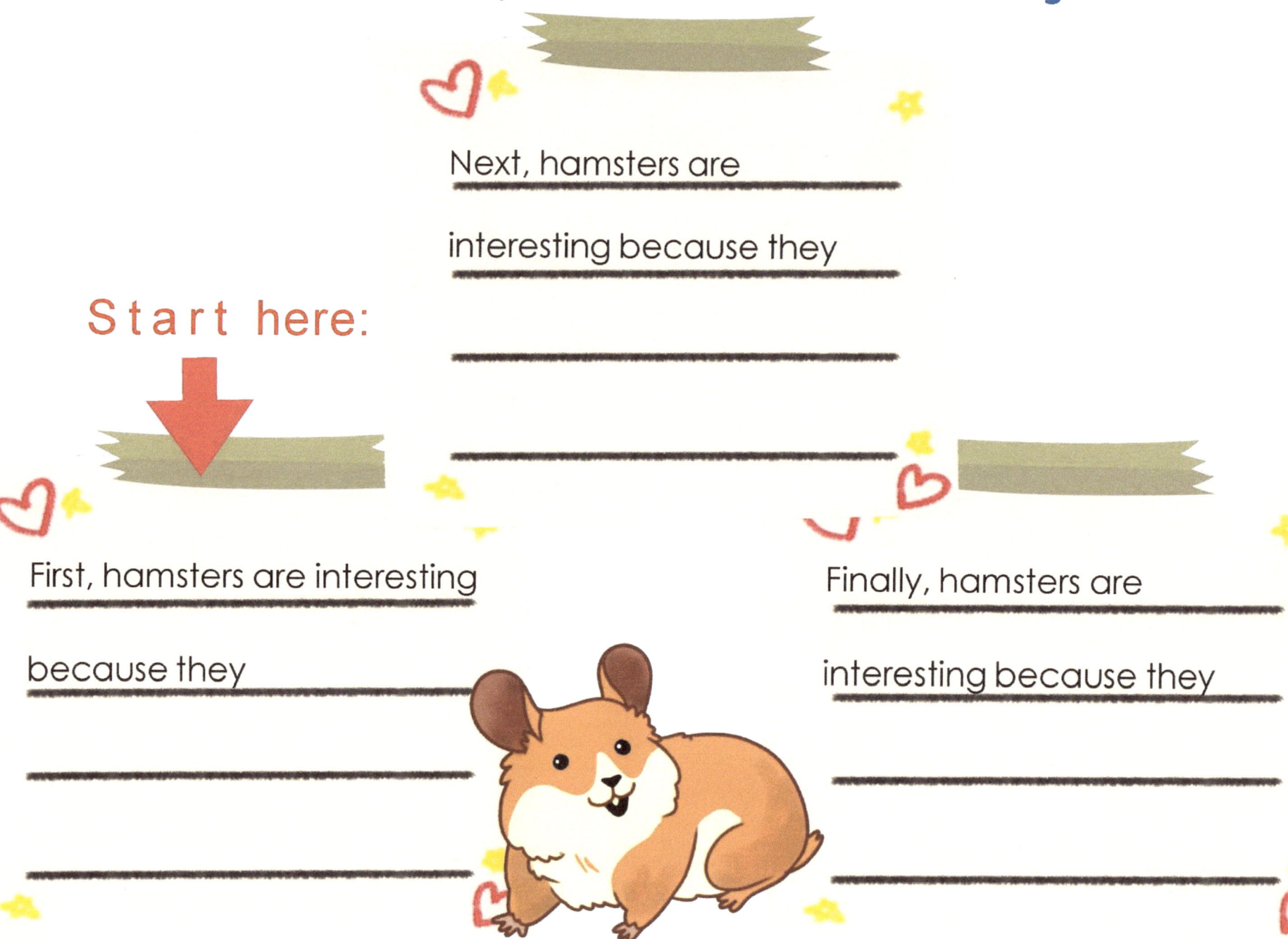

Next, hamsters are _____ interesting because they _____ _____ _____

Start here:

First, hamsters are interesting because they _____ _____ _____

Finally, hamsters are _____ interesting because they _____ _____ _____

**Why are hamsters interesting?**
Put the topic sentence and 3 reasons together.

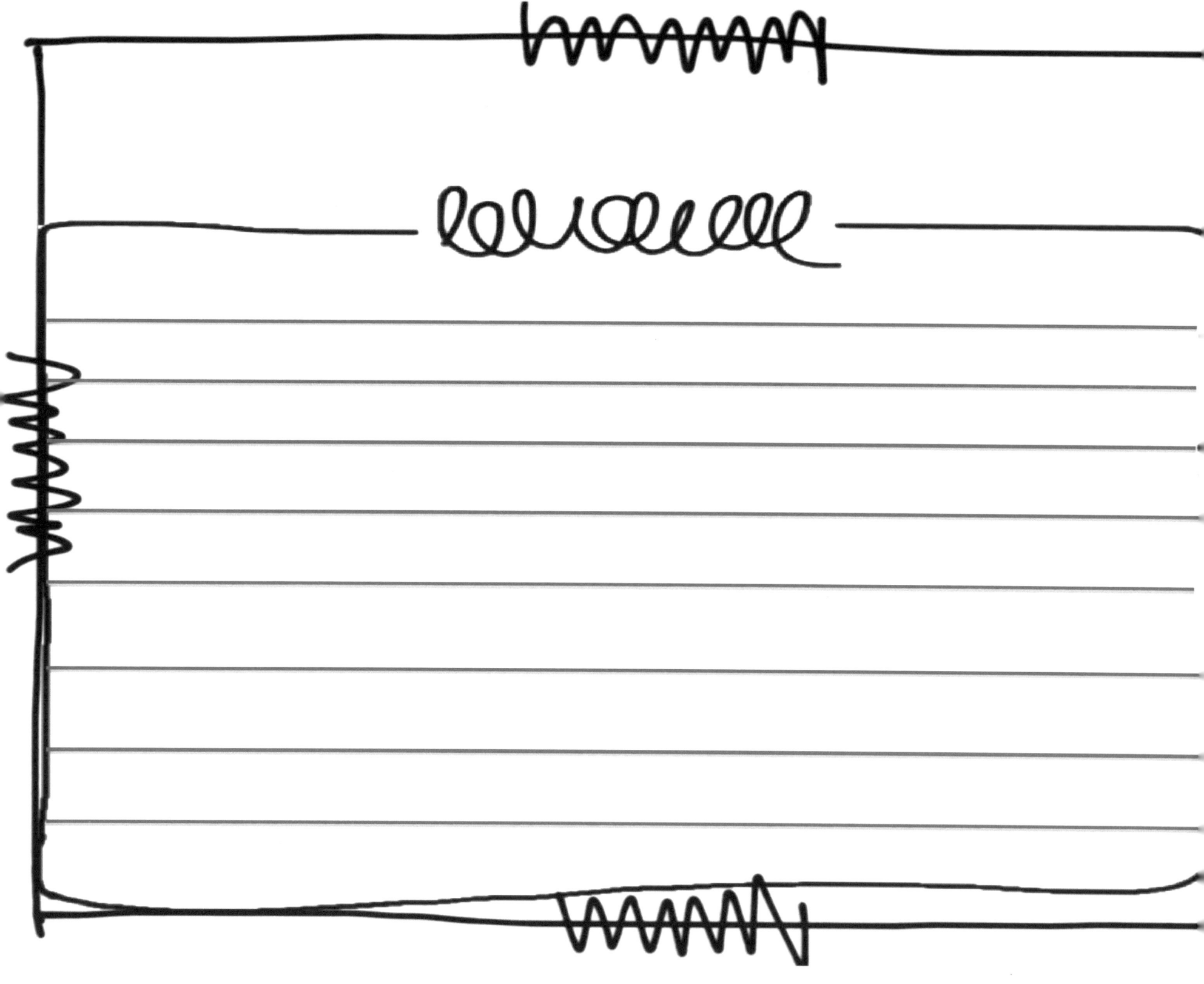

# HABITAT

An animal's habitat is where it lives.

DRAW

Wild hamsters live underground. That is their habitat (when they are not pets.)
Draw what you think their habitat looks like here.

# 2 PUG

The pug is a kind of dog.
It lives for 12 to 15 years.
Pugs are omnivores.
Stewed chicken, ground turkey, and vegetables are very healthy for pugs.
Pugs are very kind animals.
They are very nice to children.

Pugs have very strong legs.
They can play with children well because it is not easy to hurt a pug.

Pugs have two kinds of ears.
Some pugs have rose ears and some pugs have button ears.
More people like pugs with button ears.

Pugs are sleepy animals.
Pugs sleep 14 hours a day!
Do you want to have a pug for a pet?

# Lesson 2.

## Why are pugs interesting?

Try to write the topic sentence.

_____

_____

_____

Did you write the three magic words?

Now, read about pugs again.
Write 3 reasons why pugs are interesting or cool!

# Why are pugs interesting?
## Put the topic sentence and 3 reasons together.

## HABITAT

An animal's habitat is where it lives.

DRAW

Pugs do not live out in the wild. Where do pugs live? Draw their habitat here.

# Color the box next to the correct answer.

## 1. What two kinds of ears do pugs have?

☐ Some pugs have rose ears and some pugs have sunflower ears.

☐ Some pugs have rose ears and some pugs have button ears.

☐ Some pugs have round ears and some pugs have triangular ears.

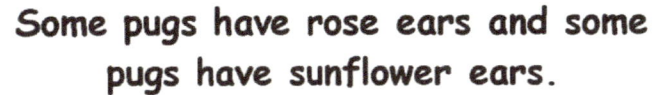

Quiz Time!

## 2. What do pugs eat?

☐ Pugs are herbivores!

☐ Pugs are omnivores!

☐ Pugs are carnivores!

# 3 Bengal cat

The Bengal Cat is a kind of pet.
Bengal Cats live for 12- 18 years.
Bengal cats have big spots and white stomachs.

All cats are carnivores.
So, the Bengal Cat is a carnivore.
Cats love to eat meat and bones.

Bengal cats are very friendly.
They like to play with other cats.
They really like to play "fighting games" with other cats.

Bengal cats are born in the wild.
So, they like to drink water from the faucet.
It makes them think of rivers and streams.

Bengal cats don't like to be lonely.
They like to sleep with other cats or with people.

Would you get a pet Bengal Cat?

## Lesson 3. Why are Bengal cats special?

Try to write the topic sentence.

Did you write the three magic words?

# Now, read about Bengal cats again.
# Write 3 reasons why Bengal cats are interesting or cool!

**Why are Bengal cats interesting?**
Put the topic sentence and 3 reasons together.

# HABITAT

An animal's habitat is where it lives.

DRAW

Bengal cats do not live out in the wild. Where do they live? Draw their habitat here.

# Color the box next to the correct answer.

### 1. Why are Bengal Cats carnivores?

- ☐ Bengal cats are carnivores because they love to eat meat and bones.

- ☐ Bengal cats are carnivores because they love to eat grass.

- ☐ Bengal cats are carnivores because they love to eat grass and meat.

*Quiz Time!*

### 2. Why are Bengal cats friendly?

- ☐ Bengal cats are friendly because they like to play with other cats.

- ☐ Bengal cats are friendly because they like to climb walls.

- ☐ Bengal cats are friendly because they like to sleep all day.

# 4 PARROT

Parrots are talking birds.
Parrots can live for 95 years.

Parrots live in tropical places.
Parrots like places that are always warm or hot and have a lot of rain.
Most parrots are herbivores. They like to eat seeds, buds, fruit, and other plant parts.

When parrots have babies, they lay eggs.
Parrot eggs are white. Parrots put their eggs in a nest.

Parrots use their feet like hands.
They pick up things with their feet and are even "right handed" and "left handed," like people. A "right handed" parrot uses its right foot to grab more things.

Scientists think parrots are the most intelligent birds.
The African Grey Parrot can make its own sentences.
Do you want a pet parrot?

## Lesson 4. Why are parrots interesting?
Put the topic sentence and 3 reasons together.

**DRAW**

Use your paragraph to draw pictures.
(Show each of your reasons.)

**FIRST,**

**NEXT,**

**FINALLY,**

## Color the box next to the correct answer.

**1. Why do parrots like living in tropical places?**

☐ Parrots like places where they can swim.

☐ Parrots like places that have a lot of snow.

☐ Parrots like places that are always warm or hot and have a lot of rain.

**2. Why are parrots herbivores?**

☐ They like to eat small fish.

☒ They like to eat seeds, buds, fruit, and other plant parts.

☐ They like to eat shrimp and fruit.

# 5 Betta fish

The real name of the Betta Fish is the "Siamese Fighting Fish." But, many people call it a Betta Fish. Betta Fish have a short life. This fish only lives for 2-4 years.

Betta fish are carnivores.
They love to eat shellfish and water insects.

Male (boy) Betta Fish love babies.
The male betta fish make a nest for eggs out of a bubble in the water. After the mommy betta fish releases eggs, the male fish chases her away, so she doesn't eat them.
Then, the male betta fish takes care of all of the eggs.

Betta fish are tropical fish.
They love to live in very hot places.

Betta Fish were named "Siamese Fighting Fish" because people in Thailand once played games by letting their fish fight each other.

Betta fish like to fight. They even open their fins to try to scare other fish. It's best to keep this fish in a bowl alone.

Do you want this fish for a pet?

**Lesson 5.**

## Why are betta fish interesting?
Remember to write the topic sentence and 3 reasons.

**DRAW**

> Use your paragraph to draw pictures.
> (Show each of your reasons.)

**FIRST,**

**NEXT,**

**FINALLY,**

# Color the box next to the correct answer.

## 1. What do betta fish eat?

- [ ] They love to eat shellfish and water insects.

- [ ] They love to eat sand.

- [ ] They love to eat plants from the ocean.

## 2. What is the betta fish's other name?

- [ ] Betta fish are also called red gold fish.

- [ ] Betta fish are also called Siamese Fighting Fish.

- [ ] Betta fish are also called tropical baby sharks.

# Word Search

Can you find the words? Circle each word in the word search.

**word list**

- betta fish
- carnivores
- love
- babies
- tropical
- thailand
- siamese
- insect
- water
- chase
- nest

```
b  e  a  u  t  i  f  u  l  l
e  n  b  c  h  a  s  e  i  o
t  v  c  s  a  t  s  e  n  v
t  r  o  p  i  c  a  l  s  e
a  o  m  l  l  a  y  e  e  b
f  h  u  g  a  z  m  g  c  a
i  c  e  s  n  i  f  e  t  b
s  f  u  n  d  c  u  p  s  i
h  g  u  b  r  e  t  a  w  e
c  a  r  n  i  v  o  r  e  s
```

# 6 rabbits

Rabbits are small mammals.
Mammals are animals that have hair or fur, have babies (not eggs), and give milk to their babies.
Boy and girl rabbits have different names.
The boy rabbit is called a "buck", the girl rabbit is called a "doe", and the baby rabbit is called a "kitten" or a "kit."

Rabbits like to live in places with grass and trees. Their habitats can be meadows, woods, forests, grasslands, deserts, and wetlands.

Pet rabbits sleep in cages. Pet rabbits usually eat fresh vegetables and drink lots of water.

Rabbits are herbivores. They eat grass and weeds. Wild rabbits do not eat carrots. They like grass more than carrots.

Rabbits live between 9 and 12 years.

Rabbits wake up very easily when sleeping.
They also sleep with their eyes open. Rabbits are very kind animals and pets.

Do you want a pet rabbit?

**Detail 3**

**Finally,** _____

_____

Draw a rabbit.

Where do wild rabbits live? Draw their habitat.

# Color the box next to the correct answer.

1. What do people call baby rabbits?

- [ ] A baby rabbit is called a "kitten" or a "kit."
- [ ] A baby rabbit is called a "doe."
- [ ] A baby rabbit is called a "bunny."

2. What do wild rabbits eat?

- [ ] Wild rabbits love to eat carrots!
- [ ] Wild rabbits love to eat broccoli.
- [ ] Wild rabbits love to eat grass and weeds.

# 7 box turtles

Most box turtles live in North America.
They like to live near fresh water.
You can find them near ponds, streams, and marshes.
Box turtles have special shells that are like caves.
They can hide inside their shells and close them when they are scared.

Boy and girl box turtles have different colored eyes.
Boy box turtles have red or orange eyes.
Girl box turtles have yellowish brown eyes.

Box turtles are omnivores.
They will eat anything they can catch!
But, baby box turtles are usually carnivores and eat mostly meat. Adult box turtles are usually herbivores and like to eat more plants.

Box turtles can live to be more than 100 years old.
But, most box turtles live to be 50 years old.

Some children have box turtles as pets. But, box turtles don't really like to be pets.

Box turtles do not like to live in new places.
Some miss their habitat and feel sad when they cannot find it.

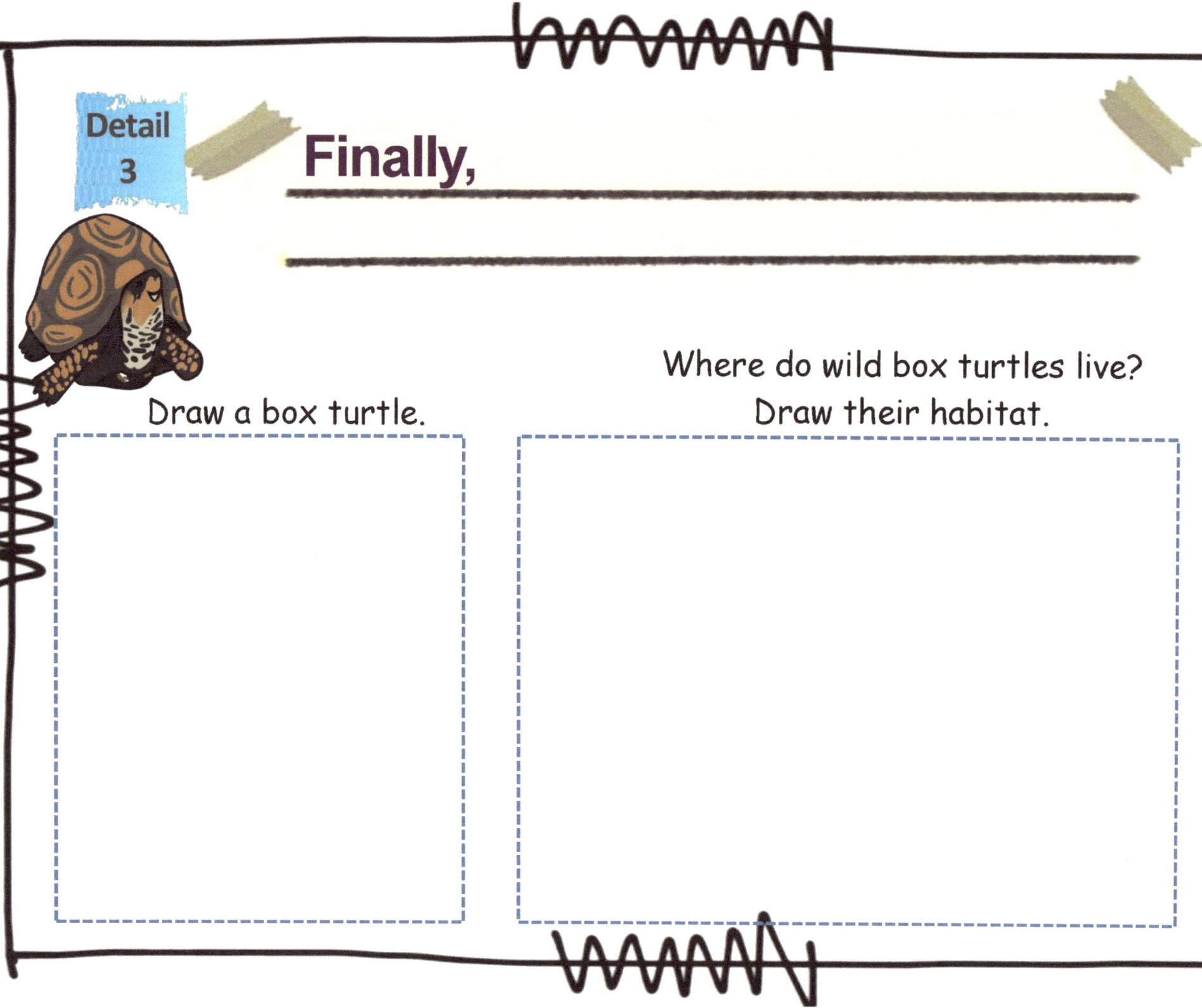

Color the box next to the correct answer.

1. Where do box turtles hide when they are scared?

☐ They hide inside their shells.

☐ They hide under water.

☐ They hide behind another box turtle.

2. What do box turtles like to live near?

☐ They like to live near the forest.

☐ They like to live near fresh water.

☐ They like to live near bee hives.

# 8 Hermit crab

Hermit crabs are crustaceans.
Crustaceans are sea animals that have a shell.

Hermit crabs are born without a shell.
But, they need a shell to live and grow strong.

Hermit crabs get shells by finding empty shells and crawling inside them. When a hermit crab gets too big for its shell, it has to find a new one.

Some hermit crabs fight each other.
If two hermit crabs want the same shell, they will fight to get it.

Some hermit crabs make a line from biggest crab to smallest crab when they find a shell.
The biggest crab can have the shell if it will fit.

Hermit crabs are friendly.
They like to live in big groups called "colonies."

Hermit crabs are omnivores.
They can eat fruit, vegetables, and cooked meat.

Hermit crabs have short lives.
They only live for a couple of months.

# Why are hermit crabs interesting?

Main Idea:

First,

Next,

Finally,

## Draw.

First

Next,

Finally,

## Color the box next to the correct answer.

1. When do hermit crabs fight one another?

  ☐ Hermit crabs never fight.

  ☐ Hermit crabs fight when they are hungry.

  ☐ If two hermit crabs want the same shell, they will fight to get it.

2. When hermit crabs are in big groups, what are they called?

  ☐ colonies

  ☐ pups

  ☐ a school

## How will you celebrate?

Today, I will _____

_____

because I did a great job and I learned to write a paragraph by myself! sign: _____

www.kidyouniversity.com

www.ingramcontent.com/pod-product-compliance
Lightning Source LLC
Chambersburg PA
CBHW041820080526

44589CB00004B/63